The Tortoise and the Birds

by Miranda Walker
Illustrated by Daniele Fabbri

OXFORD
UNIVERSITY PRESS

Chapter 1
A party on the mountain top

Long ago in Africa, the morning sun rose over a stony hillside. Slowly, slowly, Tortoise pushed his way out of his bed among the rocks. He wanted to lie in the hot sun. When his body was nice and warm, Tortoise began to think about his stomach. It was time for breakfast!

Tortoise trundled down the track in search of food, but flowers and leaves were hard to find.

"I know," he thought, "I'll ask Eagle if she's seen any tasty food growing nearby. She can see much further than me when she's flying overhead."

After a long, slow walk, Tortoise reached Eagle's tree and looked up. "Eagle!" he cried. "It's Tortoise."

Eagle peered down. She was pleased to see her friend, even if it was very early. She stretched her wings wide and glided down to greet him.

"I'm so hungry," said Tortoise, "but there's no food left on my hillside."

"I'm going to a party on the mountain top," Eagle said, smiling. "There will be plenty of food for everyone. You can come with me!"

"Oh, Eagle, I'd love to," said Tortoise, "but tortoises can't fly. I won't be able to get there."

"You will," said Eagle, "with some help from my brothers." Eagle gave a loud cry and four magnificent eagles swooped down. "Brothers," said Eagle, "will you give some of your precious feathers to Tortoise so he can fly to the party with us?"

Eagle and her kind brothers gathered around Tortoise. They each took some of their beautiful feathers and attached them to Tortoise's front legs. When their work was done, he looked very different!

"I feel peculiar," Tortoise said, clumsily flapping his new wings.

Can you think of another word Tortoise could have used instead of 'peculiar' to describe how he felt about having wings?

"You just need to get used to having feathers," said Eagle. "Now try to fly over that lake."

Tortoise trembled, but he took a few steps, flapped his new wings hard and launched himself into the air.

As he flew over the water, Tortoise looked down and caught sight of his reflection. How wonderful he looked!

Tortoise landed and puffed out his chest. "I'm more than just a tortoise now," he said to Eagle, "and more than a bird, too. From now on, you must call me Kulu. It means *all and everything*."

Chapter 2
All and everything

Tortoise was soon soaring high in the sky with Eagle and her brothers. Tortoise even overtook Eagle, until she reminded him that he didn't know the way to the party.

Eventually, they arrived. The eagles were all keen to see Kingfisher, who was the host of the party.

"Thank you for your kind invitation," said Eagle.

"What fine creature is this?" asked Kingfisher, staring at Tortoise. "Are you a tortoise or a bird?"

"Neither," replied Tortoise. "I am Kulu. I am all and everything."

"Then you must eat before everyone else," Kingfisher said, with a smile. She led Tortoise to the best table.

Eagle and her brothers were pleased to see their hungry friend treated so well.

Tortoise began to eat.

"Slow down, Tortoise," whispered Eagle, as Tortoise feasted on dish after dish. "Leave some for us!"

Tortoise frowned at his good friend and her kind brothers. "My name is Kulu," he replied crossly, "and I will eat my fill!"

The poor birds were left with nothing to eat but the scraps, scattered on the floor.

The scraps of food were scattered on the floor. Does this mean that the food was in a neat pile or that it was spread out over the floor?

After his huge meal, Tortoise fell fast asleep. The eagles could hardly hear his snores over the sound of their rumbling stomachs.

"I'm sorry," Eagle said to her brothers. "You gave up your feathers so my hungry friend could eat. Now we're the hungry ones."

"It is not your fault," said one of the brothers. He shook his head sadly. "Tortoise has become boastful and selfish. No one is *all and everything*."

"We could take our feathers back," suggested another brother. "Then Kulu will be plain old Tortoise again."

Chapter 3
How to get home

After a long, deep sleep, Tortoise began to stir. When he opened his eyes, he was surprised that he was not at home on his hillside. Then he remembered. He wasn't Tortoise any more. He was Kulu!

Nearby, a duck looked at Tortoise curiously. Tortoise decided to show off. He stretched out his impressive wings … but nothing happened! He looked down in alarm. Where had his feathers gone? He looked around. They weren't anywhere to be found.

"Duck," said Tortoise, waving one of his legs, "have you seen my feathers?"

"Well, I saw you fly here with feathers, given to you by your friends," said Duck.

"Yes, but where are my feathers now?" demanded Tortoise.

"Then I saw you eat all the food and leave your friends with only scraps," continued Duck.

"I was hungry!" snapped Tortoise.

"*Then* you fell asleep," said Duck. "That's when I saw the eagles take their feathers back and fly home with the other guests."

"They removed my feathers?" said Tortoise, alarmed. "How ever will I get home? I can't fly without them!"

Tortoise is told the eagles removed his feathers. Can you think of a different way of saying 'removed'?

"Don't look at me," said Duck. "I can't carry a heavy tortoise."

"I am not a tortoise," came the reply. "I am Kulu. I am all and everything!"

Just then, Kingfisher flew past. Tortoise remembered how much he had impressed Kingfisher. She was bound to help him!

"Kingfisher!" Tortoise called. "It's Kulu. I need a lift down the mountain."

Kingfisher <u>glared</u> at the featherless creature. "Don't be ridiculous! You're not Kulu. He has magnificent wings. You're a tortoise. You will have to make your own way down the mountain." With that, Kingfisher was gone.

Kingfisher <u>glared</u> at Tortoise. Can you show this expression on your face?

Tortoise started to worry. He had to get back home somehow. He thought long and hard. There was only one way …

"Duck," he said, "I'm going to jump down from the mountain."

Duck was surprised. "Are you sure that's a good idea?" he asked.

Tortoise nodded. "I've got to try. Now, fly down ahead of me and pile up lots of soft things for me to land on: leaves, grass, whatever you can find."

"That sounds like a lot of work," replied Duck.

"I am Kulu. I am all and everything. Now do as I say!" demanded Tortoise.

Duck flew away.

Chapter 4
Friends once more

Tortoise felt very lonely as he waited. He wasn't sure how long it would take Duck to prepare his nice soft landing.

As time passed, he wondered if Duck would help him at all. He couldn't remember if he had even said *please*.

Tortoise decided that he had waited long enough. His heart filled with dread, but he took a deep breath, then jumped bravely into the sky.

As Tortoise fell, he realized he hadn't been a very good friend to the eagles, although they had helped him.

Why did Tortoise's heart fill with dread? What was he worried might happen when he jumped?

Tortoise hurtled down towards the ground ... and began to panic. He looked desperately for the soft pile of leaves, but it was nowhere to be seen. What would happen to him now?

Suddenly, he didn't want to be Kulu. He didn't want to be all and everything any more.

Tortoise decided that as soon as he reached the ground, he would say sorry to Eagle and her brothers.

With a big bump, Tortoise landed on the ground the wrong way up, cracking his beautiful shell.

Tortoise dusted himself off and slowly, slowly made his way to Eagle's tree.

"Eagle!" he cried. "It's your friend, Tortoise. I'm not Kulu any more. I'm very, very sorry. I realize how my selfishness <u>affected</u> you and your brothers."

How did Tortoise's actions <u>affect</u> Eagle and her brothers?

Eagle swooped down. "I can see you have learned your lesson," she said.

Eagle and Tortoise became friends once more.

Then Eagle carefully glued Tortoise's broken shell back together. "You know," said Eagle, "I like the new pattern on your shell."

Eagle pointed to the shiny lake. "Go on," she encouraged, "have a look."

Tortoise took a deep breath. Then he stuck out his neck and took a good, long look at his reflection.

Finally, he smiled. Tortoise liked his new shell very much.

Since that day, every single tortoise has been born with a beautiful, cracked-looking shell, and every single eagle chick has been told the story of *The Tortoise and the Birds*. It helps them to remember to be kind to their friends.

Read and discuss

Read and talk about the following questions.

Page 7: Can you imagine how <u>peculiar</u> it would be to suddenly have wings? What do you think it would feel like?

Page 13: What might you <u>scatter</u> on the ground for birds to eat? Can you show how you would <u>scatter</u> it?

Page 19: What did Eagle and her brothers <u>remove</u> from Tortoise? Why did they do this?

Page 21: How do you think Tortoise felt when Kingfisher <u>glared</u> at him? Do you think Tortoise deserved it?

Page 25: Can you think of some other words that you could use instead of the word '<u>dread</u>'?

Page 28: Which other characters in the story were <u>affected</u> by Tortoise's actions?